PHEASANT TRA

Copyright © 2019 by Malcolm Bowler. All rights reserved. This book or any portion thereof may not be reproduced or used in any manner whatsoever without the express written permission of the author except for the use of brief quotations in a book review.

Disclaimer: The information contained within this Book is strictly for educational purposes. If you wish to apply ideas contained in this Book, you are taking full responsibility for your actions.

Contents

Introduction

Cages and net frames

Funnel pheasant traps

Pheasant pit trap

Arapuca trigger pheasant trap

Paiute trigger pheasant trap

Coop trap

Figure 4 pheasant trap

Net traps

Baits

Fools cap trap

Stove pipe trap

string pheasant trap

Snares

Other cage traps

This book is in no way encouraging the illegal trapping of pheasants , it is a book of reference for those who are interested in trapping and trap building in modern times and the old days . Pheasants in the UK are regarded as property so unless you have permission from whoever owns them you cannot kill or keep them , in the book are some traps that would definitely be illegal and they have been kept in the book to make it complete , most of the traps mentioned are old world techniques and methods , that you rarely see today but all are very interesting nonetheless .

Trying to find out info about who made and used these type of traps is very vague , most are techniques from a long time ago , but no doubt gamekeepers and poachers would have used them , from the info i could find it seems most of the cage type traps would have been used by gamekeepers for rounding up stray birds and snares and other traps would have been used by poachers .

Also pheasants are found all around the world and many of the indigenous people would have definitely trapped them as well, so i suspect some of the traps are a variation of gamekeeper , poacher and primitive trap.

Cages and net frames

Cages for deadfall type triggers were made from many things, the following pages will show a few ideas , stacked logs or square battens made a good pyramid cage stacked up like a log cabin and tied or nailed or screwed together , other cages were made from chicken wire by making a square frame of wood then covering the top with chicken wire and shaping into a dome so it forms a cage, ordinary boxes made of wood or even strong plastic will make a good cage but they lack the ability to see what has been caught unless a window or door was added and covered with fine mesh or chicken wire , all the cages unless already heavy enough needed a weight to be added so the animal didn't lift the cage.

Net frames were made by simply making a square wooden frame about 30 x 30 inches and covering the top with a loose netting, binding around the frame to hold the net on or they would add a bent stick or bit of wire over the frame to hold the net up . with framed nets the wood must be heavy as the net will not add any weight to the trap .

wooden cage

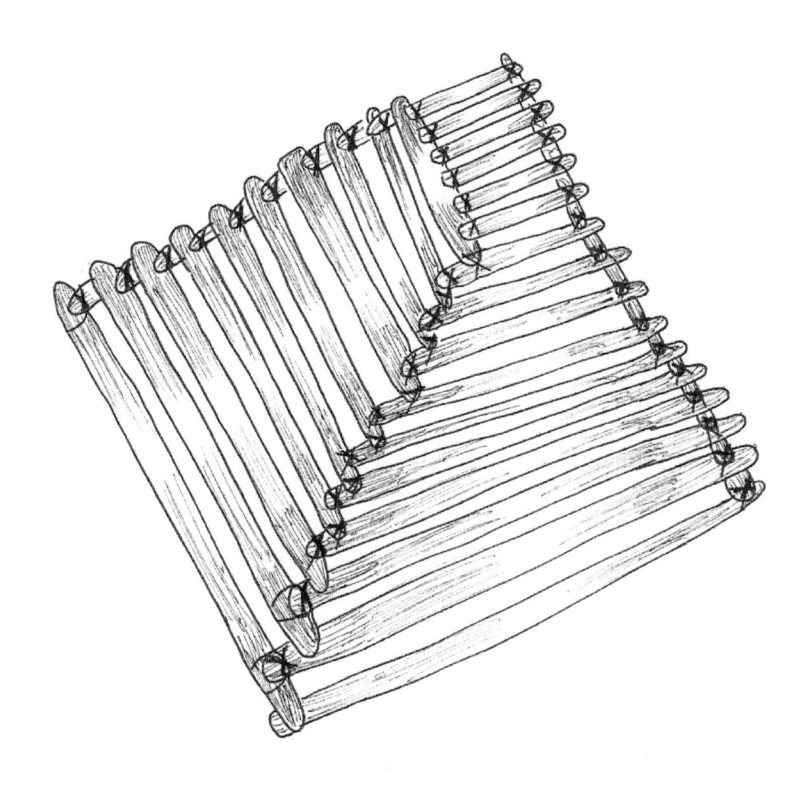

Another simple log cabin type cage was made by tying 2 strings to 2 sticks as shown in the pictures starting from top left , once 2 strings are tied to the 2 sticks you then crossed them over , now you simply start adding sticks alternating each side you add them and keep pushing them under the string each time as you go, the sticks you add will make the string get tighter and tighter eventually you can no longer add any more sticks and the whole lot will be held tightly together .

wooden cage

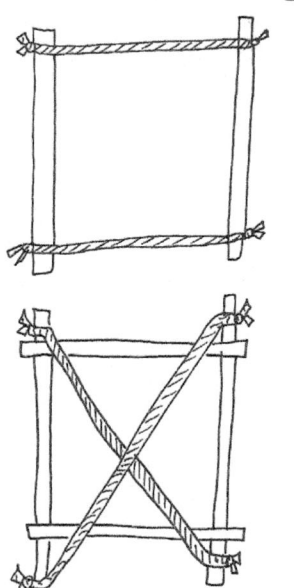

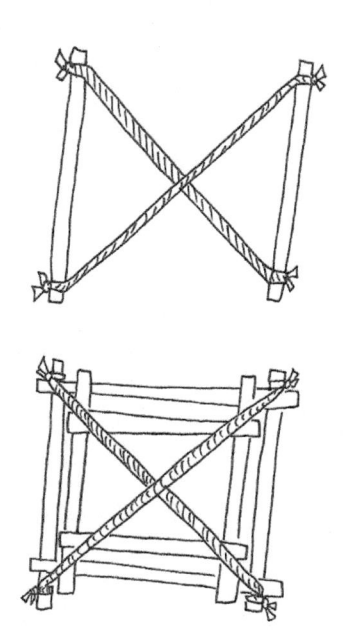

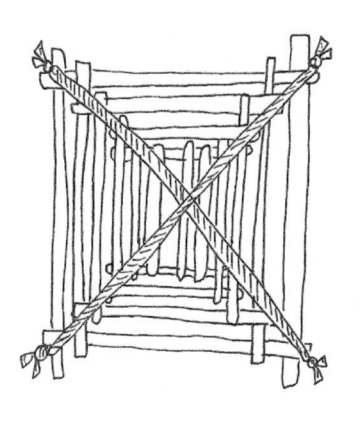

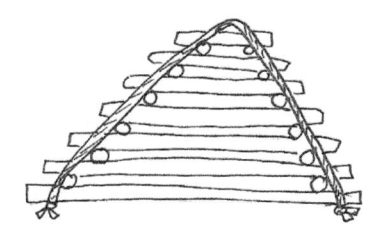

Wooden batten cage

Stacked stick cage with a hatch on top

Chicken wire cage

A very effective cage was made by making a frame of heavy wood 30 inch x 30 inch and covering the top with domed chicken wire, to make attaching the wire to the frame easier they nailed battens over the chicken wire to hold it down

NET FRAME

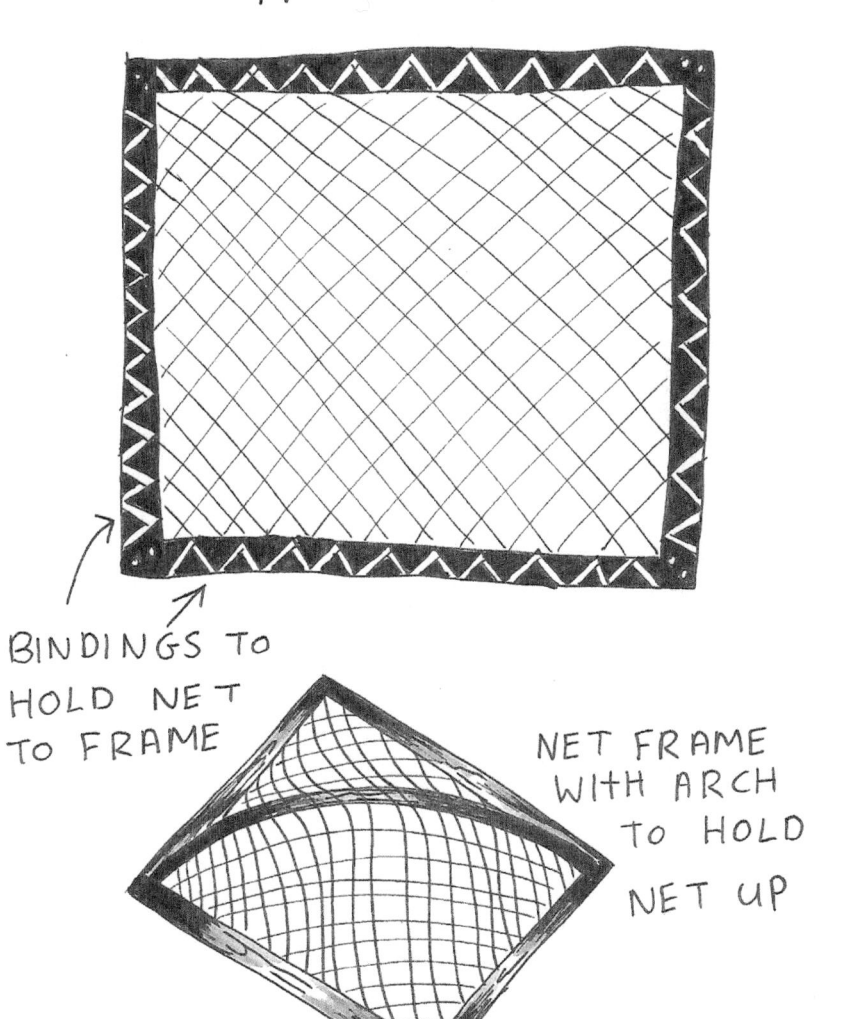

BINDINGS TO HOLD NET TO FRAME

NET FRAME WITH ARCH TO HOLD NET UP

Funnel pheasant trap

The pheasant funnel was made with some chicken wire, 4 long stakes and about 8 wooden pegs , 4 stakes were hammered / pushed into the ground in a square and chicken wire wrapped around it having the 2 ends flapping inwards as shown in the pictures, then pegs are placed all round it to keep it from being lifted ,the height of the one pictured is about 1 and a 1/2 foot tall, 3 -4 foot long and about 2-3 foot wide , they would then bind or tie any other bits if needed , the funnel part just needs a few inches at the top to be bound / weaved together , leaving an opening of about a foot , bait goes in the trap and they made sure to put bait going through the funnel / doorway, once the pheasant pushes its way in it can't find the way out again

TOP VIEW

PEGS

CHICKEN WIRE

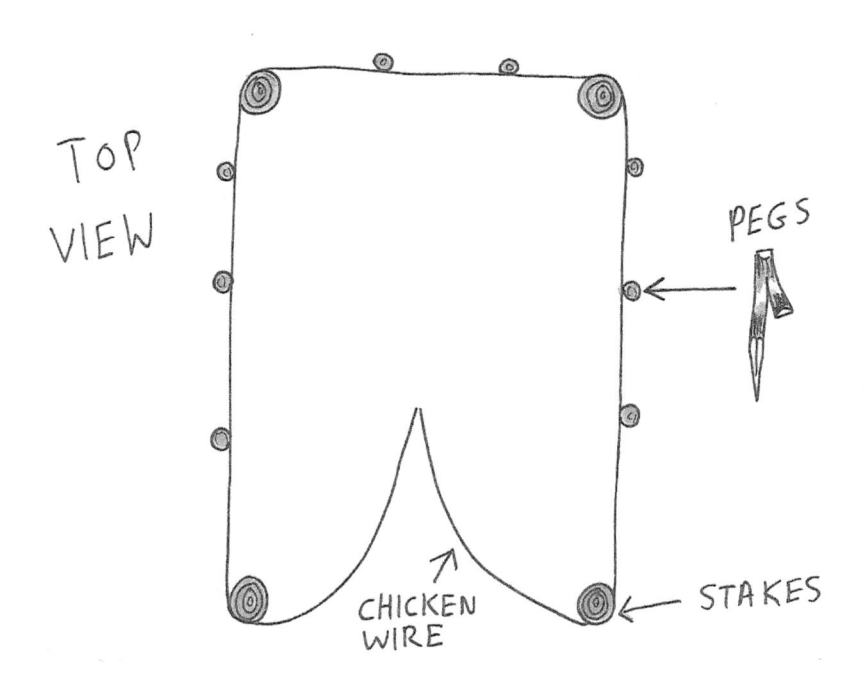

STAKES

FRONT VIEW

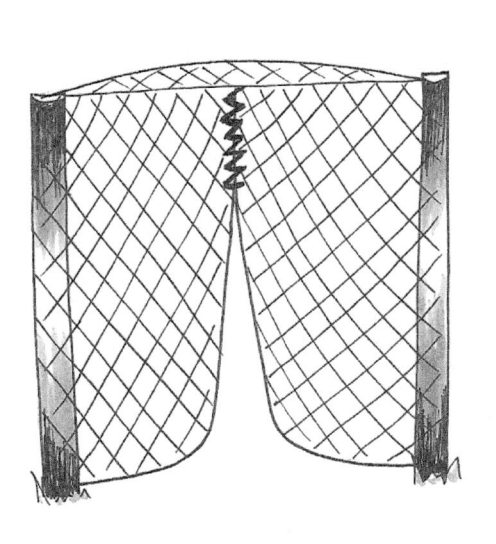

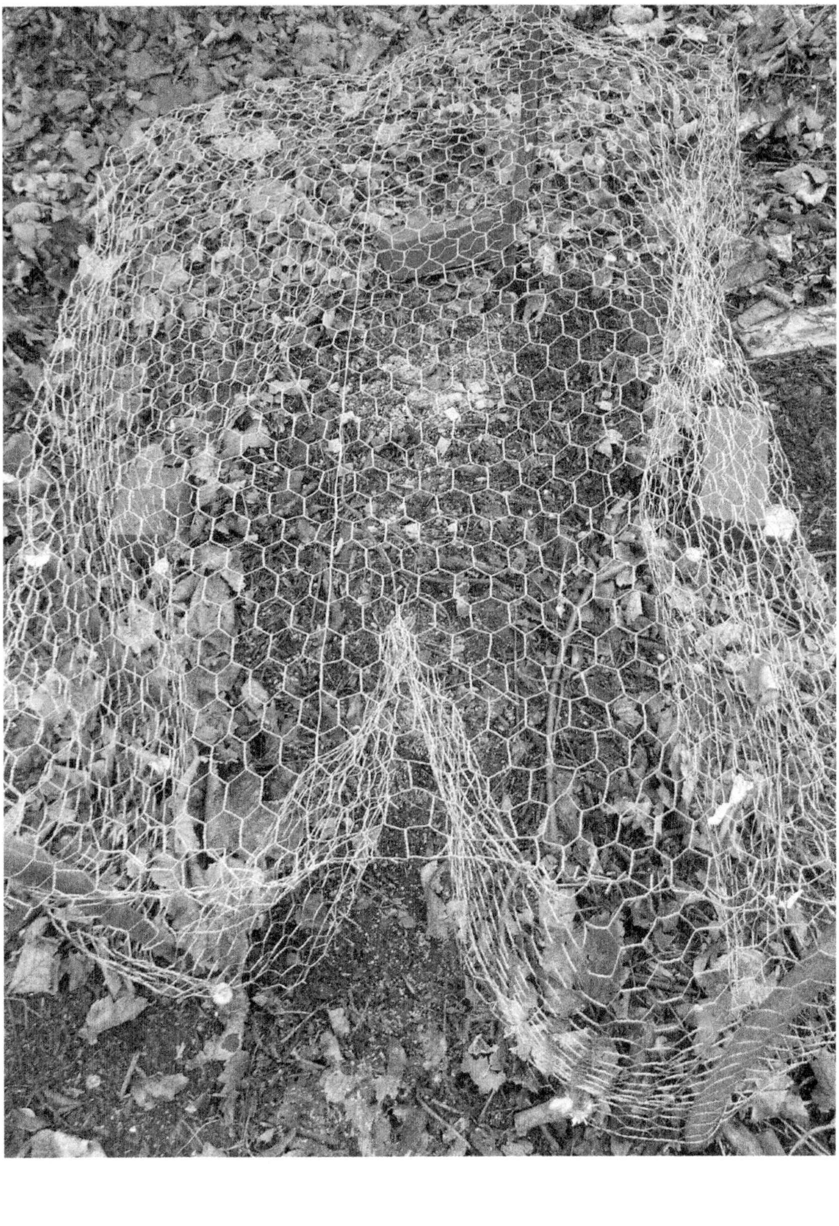

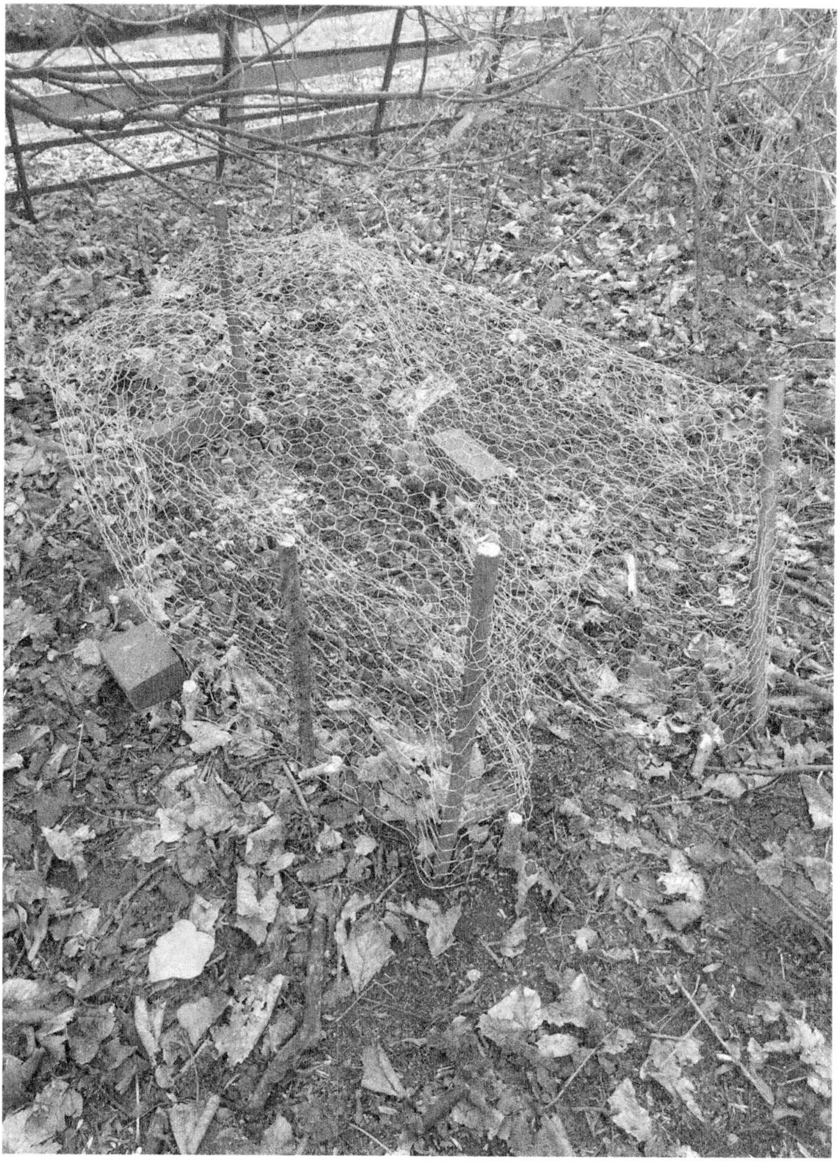

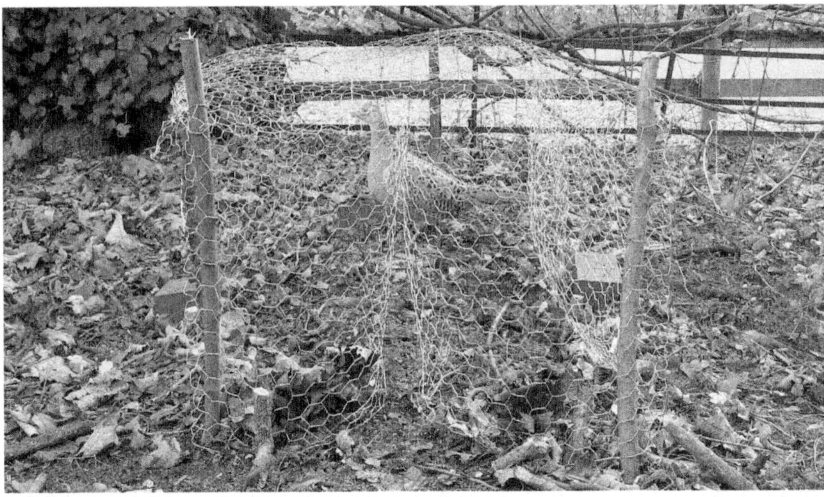

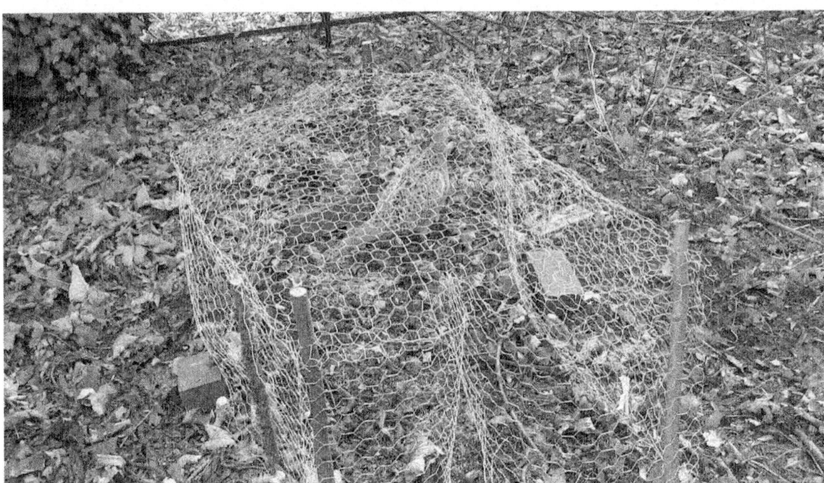

This pheasant funnel trap works the same as a funnel fish trap , a simple tube or box was made from chicken wire and a funnel or a flap is made at one end ,the entry hole was about 12 -14 inches in height and the cage part about 2-3 feet long, they formed a cone or a flap in the entrance with a hole about 8-9 inches roughly for the small end of the cone (sometimes it was smaller). The back of the trap is folded and tied with string, so it can be unfolded and the bird removed . Bait is placed at the entrance and throughout the trap with a load of bait at the back . stakes placed through the trap at the sides steadied it and held it in place ,

The bird will be able to push its way into the trap but once inside will not be able to find its way out again .

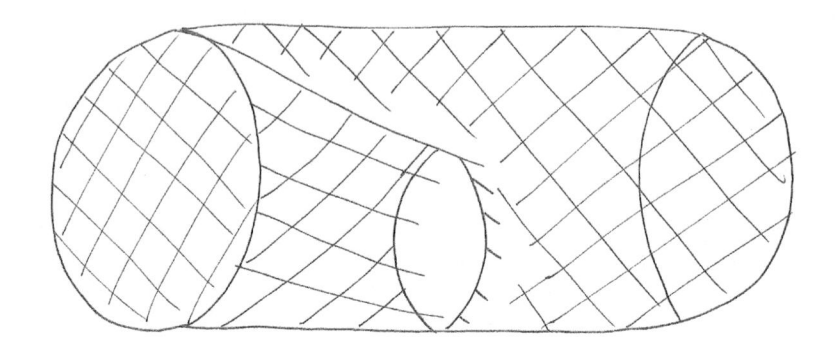

Simple diagram of the funnel trap

Pheasant pit trap

The pheasant pit trap is essentially an arapuca bird trap but set in a pit (in the next chapter i will give all the details about the trigger) being set in a pit means they didn't have to build a cage as they could just use a wooden board but something like wire mesh is better as they could can see what was inside the trap , a pit is dug about 30 x 30 inches and about 1 foot or more deep , then a board or mesh sheet is set over it and held up by an arapuca trigger, bait goes at the back between the v sticks of the trigger , when the pheasant gets down into the pit to eat the bait it knocks the trigger and down comes the lid , rocks or weights etc are placed on top of the lid to hold it down.

ARAPUCA TRIGGER ON NEXT CHAPTER .

PIT TRAP

BOARD/MESH

20

21

22

Arapuca trigger pheasant trap

The arapuca trigger pheasant trap is essentially the same as any other arapuca bird trap but with a wire cage, in the old days they would also use the pyramid of sticks cage with this trap too or any similar improvised cage . the trigger of the trap consists of 4 sticks, only 1 notch was required, the notch is carved into the vertical stick (1) so the angled stick (2) has a place to fit into to hold it up , which then holds the cage up, this in turn is held up by the angled stick forcing it to be pushed forward , the vertical stick is held back by the 2 sticks at the bottom (3), which are angled into the corners of the cage

This trap works when the animal stands on or knocks away one of the 2 sticks at the bottom and the cage will fall and trap the animal ,baits goes at the back between the 2 triggers sticks .

TOP VIEW

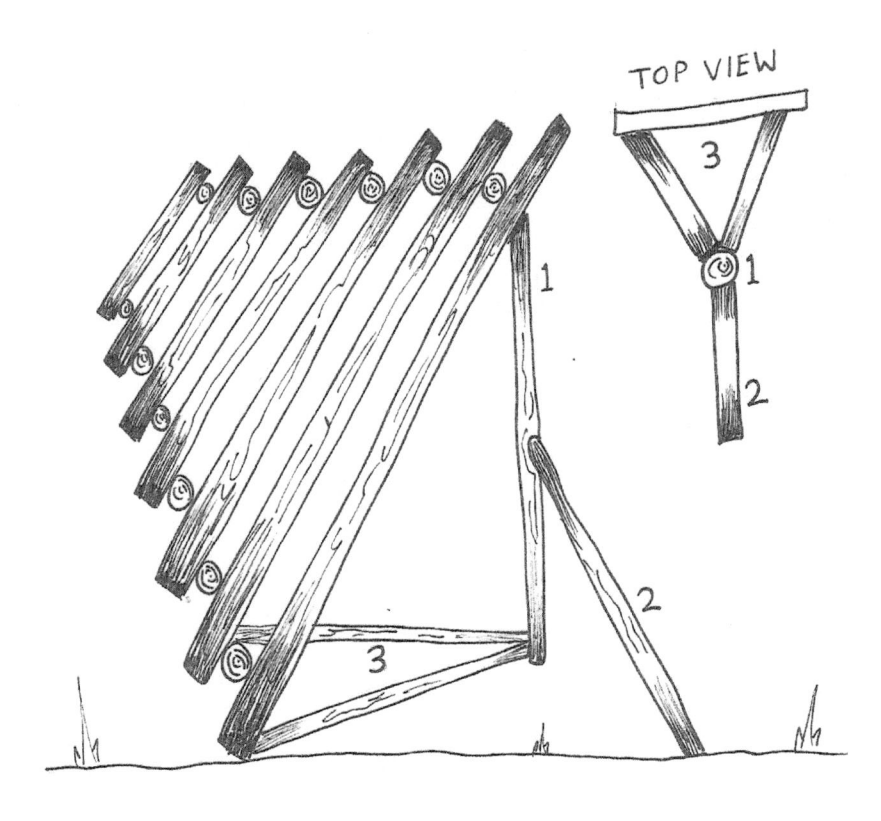

25

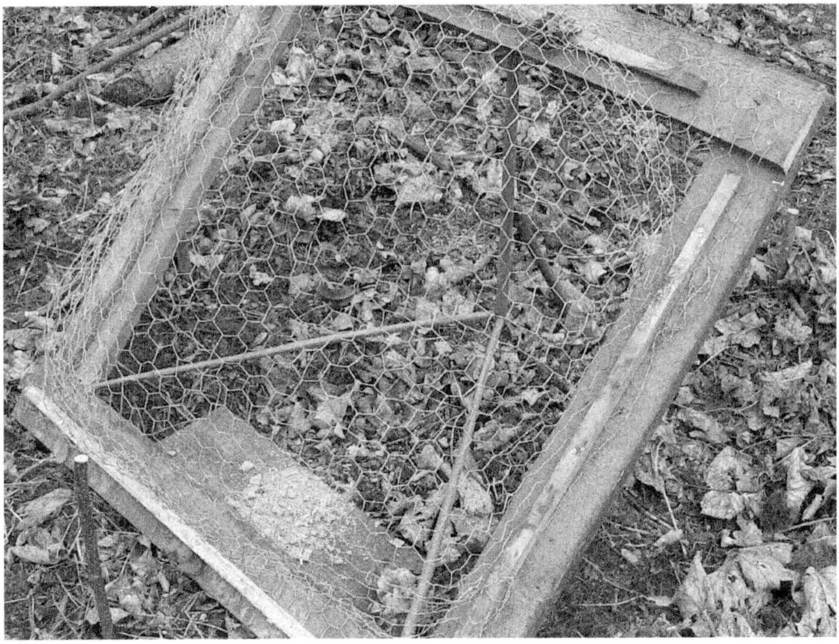

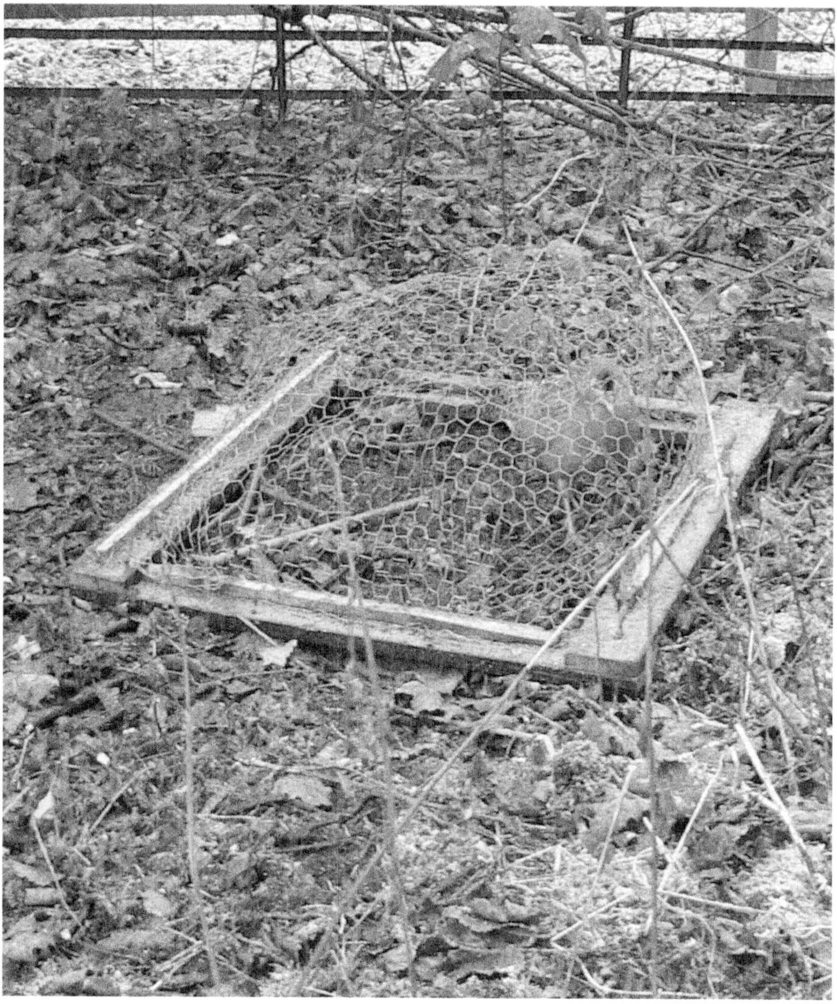

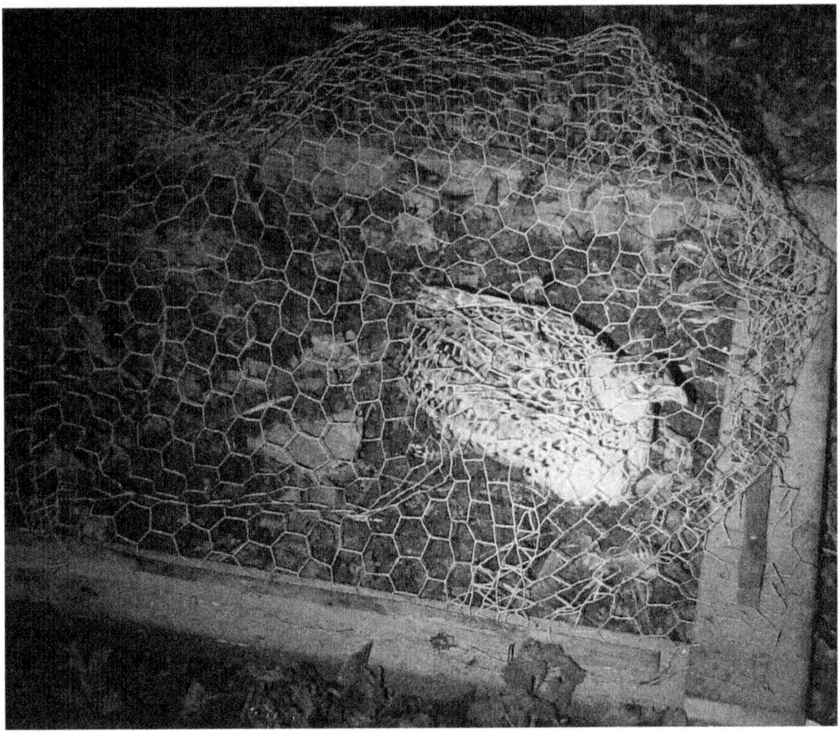

Paiute trigger pheasant trap

Any cage or net frame would have worked with this trigger , the upright stick was carved to a flat point at the top, then the top stick is placed onto it so that it pivots, then a mark is made where the ideal pivoting point is and a small notch is cut there, at the other end to where the cage will sit tie a string and take the string from the top stick to the upright stick, near the bottom the trapper would mark this and tie a small toggle here, now a long thin stick was placed between the back of the cage and toggle , bait is placed near the trigger stick, and when a bird stands on it, it releases the trigger and the cage comes down.

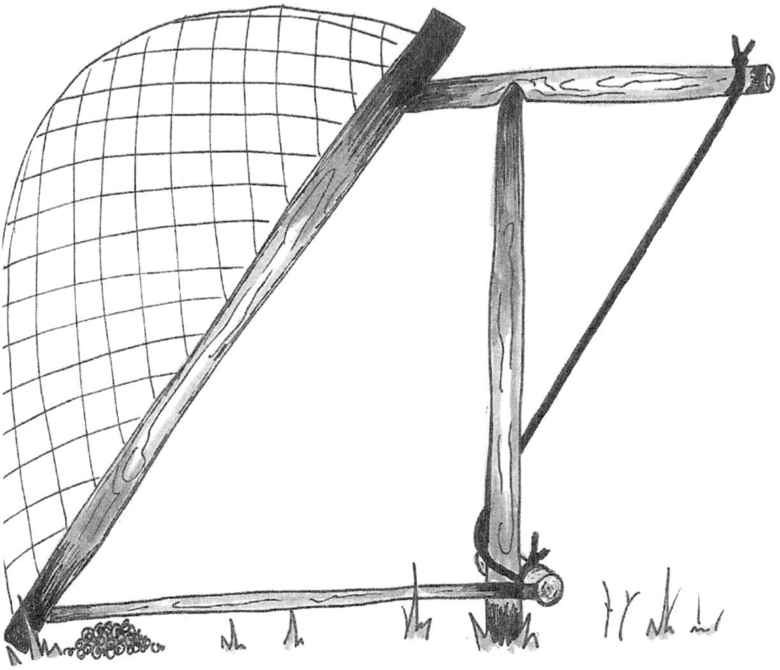

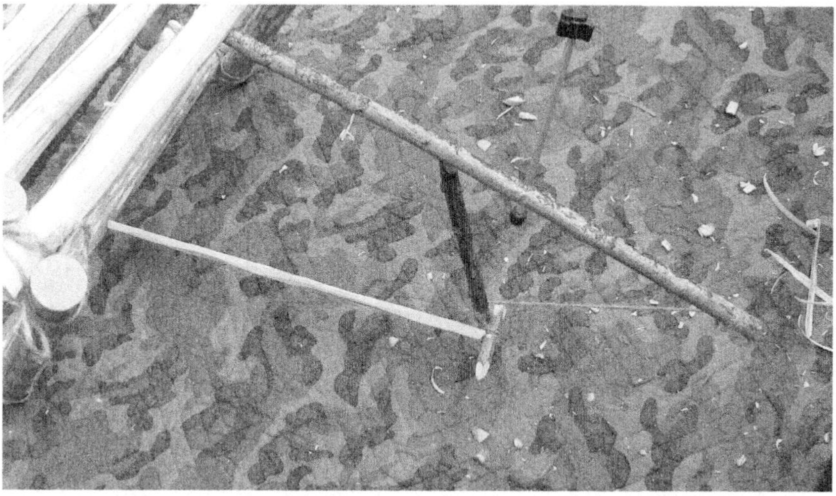

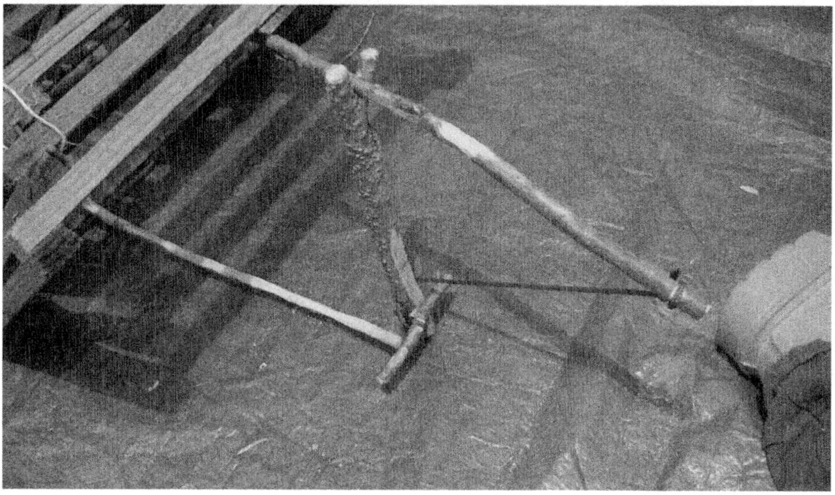

Coop trap

The coop trap also known as the turkey trap because this trap was originally used for catching turkeys in the USA. but it could be scaled down to catch most birds including pheasants and pigeons , in the old days they would simply dig a trench about the same length as their intended cage, the width of the trench will be about half the width of what the cage is and as deep as the trench is wide (they could adjust these sizes to suit their intended quarry if need be) , once the trench is dug they would either lay a suitable cage halfway over the trench as shown in the pictures , or would make a cage from stacked logs ,wood etc , once set up add bait such as seeds , nuts etc into the trench and in the cage too , some people used to add loose leaves as well , amazingly the bird can walk into the trench and duck under into the cage but once inside it cannot find its way back out again, if they added leaves this can help too as the bird may scratch around and fill the trench with the loose leaves causing more confusion as to where the entrance has gone .

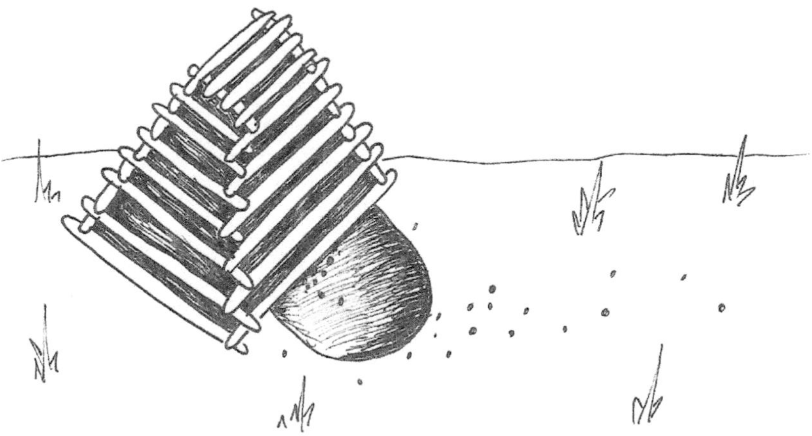

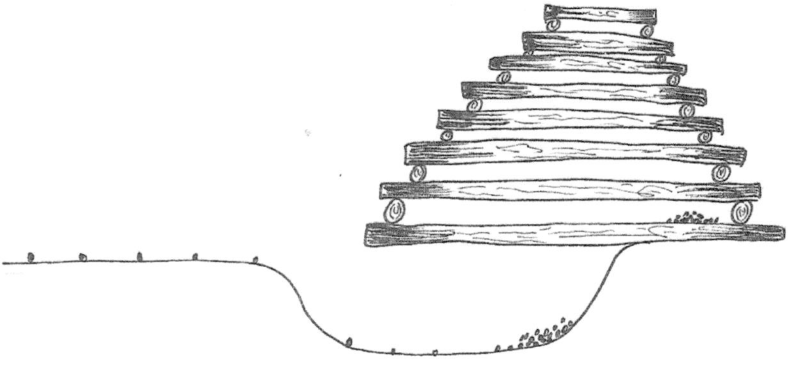

Metal cage coop trap

Stacked stick coop trap

Figure 4 pheasant trap

The figure 4 is an old trigger but very useful nonetheless , the key to making it work good was to make sure it went off easily and that the trigger is as far back into the cage so the pheasant doesn't have time to jump out of the way once it goes off , there are many different ways to make the figure 4 trigger but i'll show the most common variant . the upright stick and the trigger / bait stick needed to have 2 square notches cut into it so they fit together as pictured then cut the top of the upright stick to a flat point, then at the outside end of the trigger stick they cut a notch into it to accept the back end of the slanting stick, now they put the upright stick and the trigger stick on the floor together how they would be set, then laid the slanting stick where it's meant to go and marked the areas to cut a flat point at one end (to fit into the back end of trigger stick) and another cut to fit it to the top of the upright stick , hopefully the pictures will make sense of it , they made sure everything wasn't really tight otherwise the trap may not go off when the trigger is touched, bait is placed around the trigger stick so the pheasant knocks or stands on it , make sure the trigger stick reaches far into the back of the cage for a better catch .

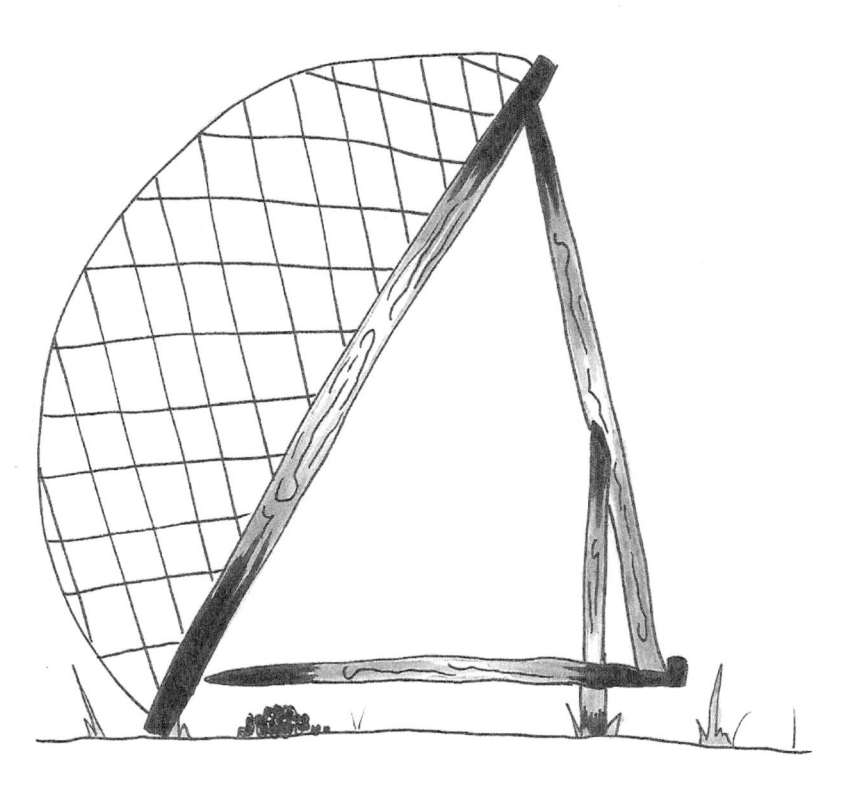

A GOOD FIGURE 4 TRIGGER
FOR PHEASANTS

Parts of the figure 4 trigger

From left to right , slanting stick ,upright stick and horizontal stick (trigger stick).

Figure 4 trap with a forked branch trigger

Framed net traps

A framed net is essentially a wooden frame with a loose net set over it and bound to the frame with string , the good thing about net frames is they were very easy to make and they could be used with many of the deadfall type triggers , if they wanted the frame to more resemble a cage they added a bendy stick or a bit of wire arched over the top of the frame to hold the net up , with a net frame heavy wood must be used otherwise the pheasant will jump up and get free from the frame or run off with the frame over it .

A quickly set up figure 4 net trap , it would be better to have the trigger stick lower down and longer if trapping pheasants .

Framed net trap , the string is over a branch and goes down to the net frame, on the other end of the string is the trigger as shown in the pictures when the pheasant knocks the stick the net frame comes falling down .

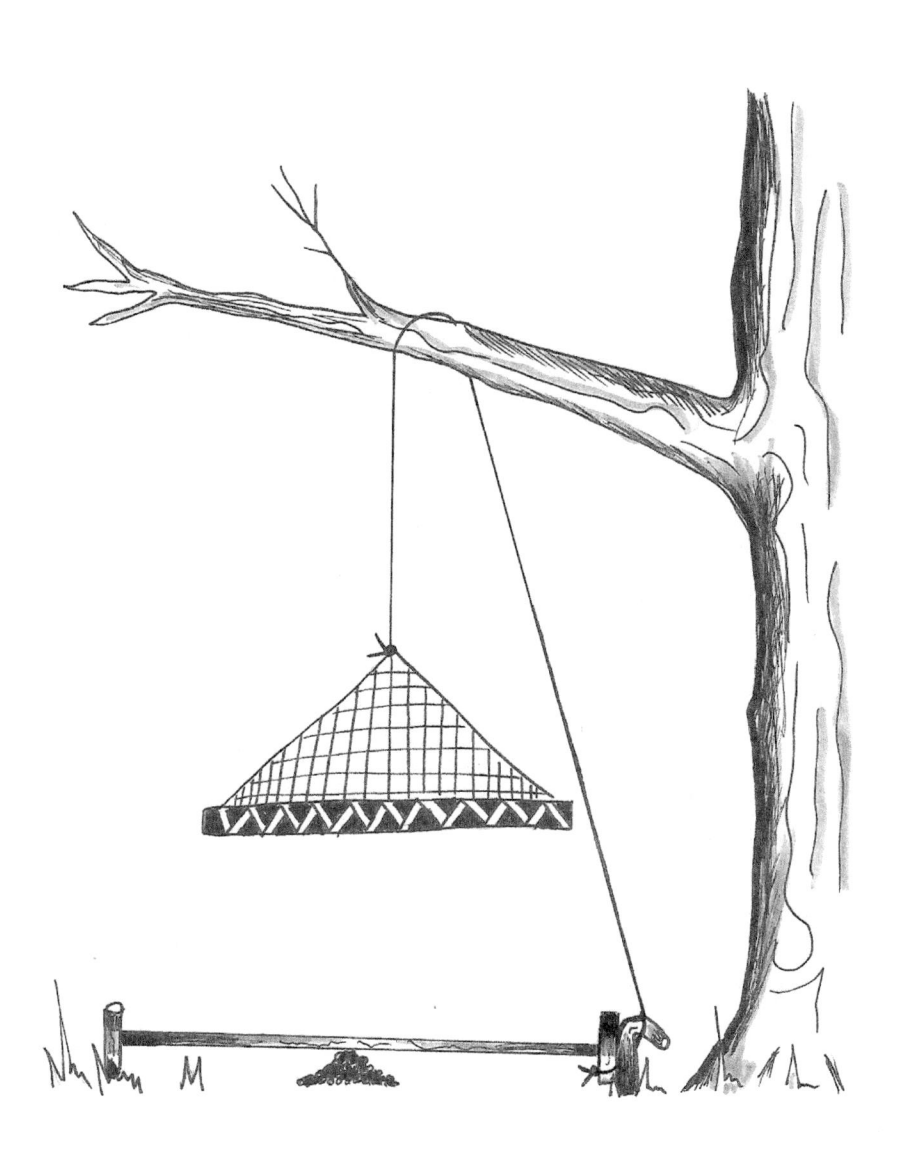

Drop framed net trap

Another very old trap , i first read about this in a book written in the late 1800s. A square wooden frame is made and a loose net is attached to it , then 4 flexible poles are pushed in the ground slightly leaning inwards as shown, 2 of the sticks needed a nail hammered through them near the top , the exposed end of the nail is pointing inwards , this is for the framed net to sit on, the other side is held by the pressure of the other sticks, 2 strings are tied to the 2 poles with the nails and these 2 are tied to single string to an area where the trapper is hidden , bait is placed directly under the net , when a birds enters the area they pulled the string which releases the net and down it comes , being a framed net it won't matter if it flips as it will work no matter what way the framed net lands .

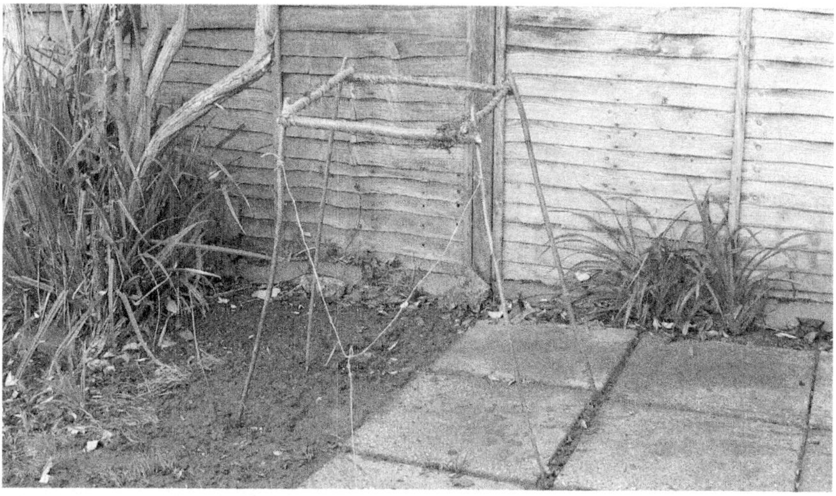

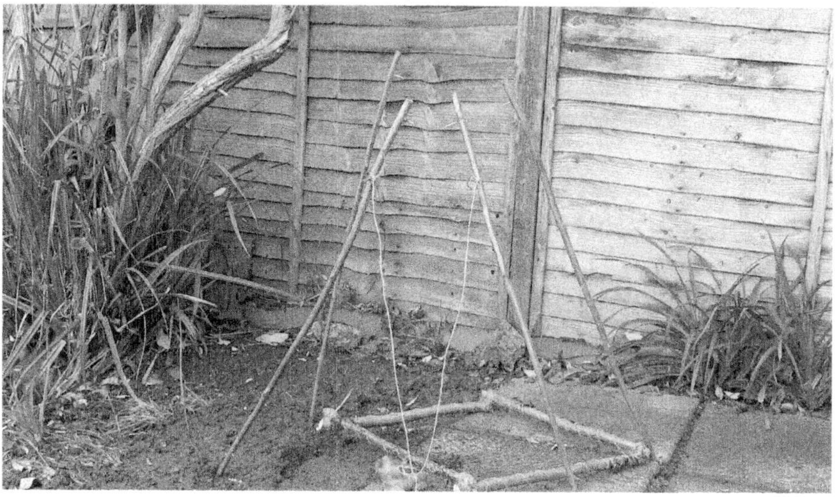

Framed net trap

This is one of the most simplest traps they made, the only other way to make it more simple was to use a box or cage, but by using a net the birds are less likely to be afraid to stand under it , a frame is made exactly the same as the last trap, and it is propped up by a stick with a string attached (in the picture the string is at the top but it may be better to have the string at the bottom) bait is put under the net and when a bird enters the trapper pulled the string and the net comes down

Many baits were used but location of the trap seems more vital than any bait, if they could find out where the birds hung about any bait seemed to work.

Improvised baits:

Sweetcorn / corn

Crushed breakfast cereals

Peas

Rice

Berries

Nuts and seeds

Bread

Chopped fruit and veg

Raisins

Crushed biscuits

Broken up cake

Bird seed

The fools cap / cone trap

The cone trap or fools cap trap , is a cone of stiff card or something similar , to get a good sized cone the trapper would draw the largest circle they could on an A4 sized piece of card or birch bark or whatever they had to hand, they then folded it in half and half again until they had a cone , then they would glue or peg the cone so it didn't unfold , they then put something sticky in the cone like treacle , honey , pine pitch , bird lime, syrup etc and added seeds or corn to this like in the pictures . they then made a hole in the ground so the cone sits flush or just above ground and added a few more seeds etc as bait , the idea of this trap is the bird will peck into the cone and the sticky substance they put inside will stick to the birds feathers and cover its head with the cone , the bird will be temporarily blinded and should stay around until trapper would come to pick it up .

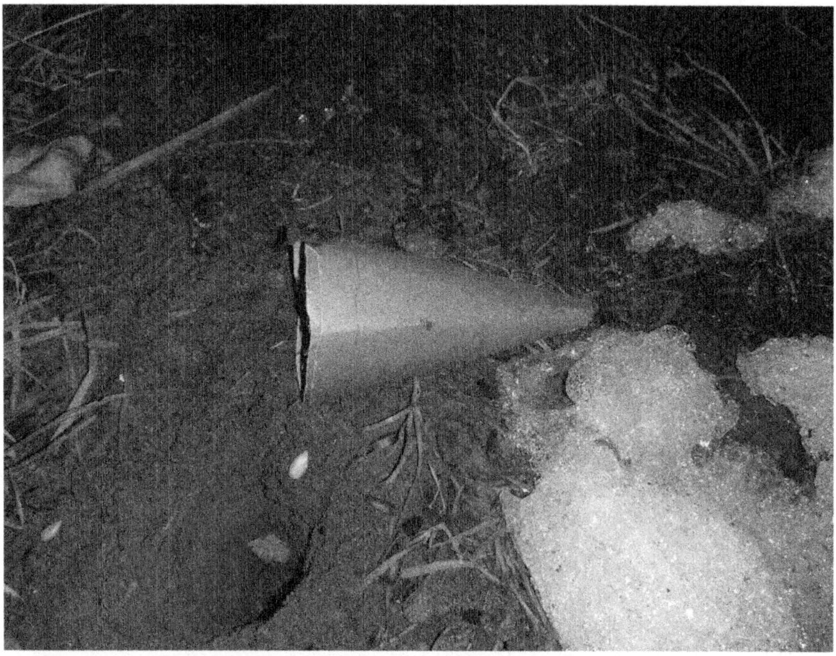

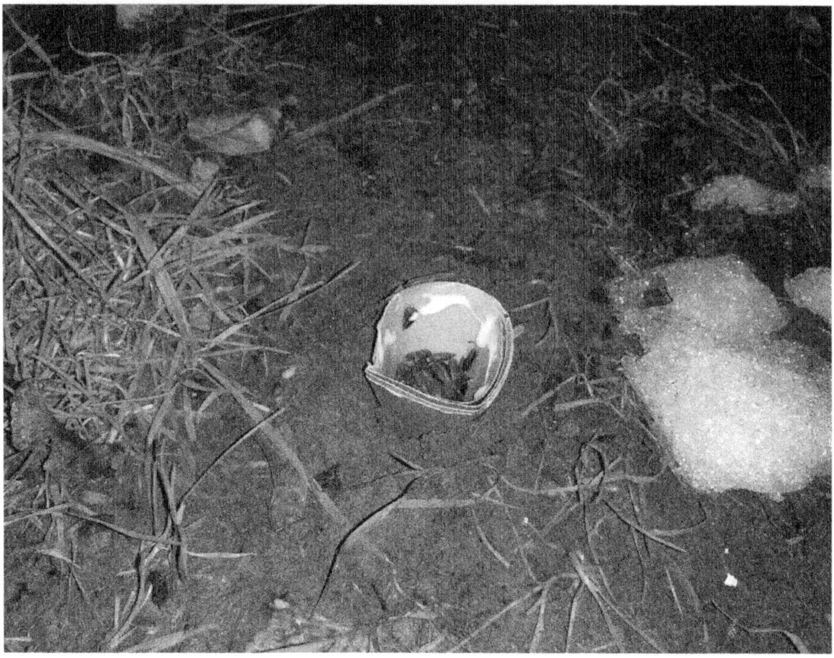

FOOLS CAP/CONE TRAPS
SET IN THE GROUND

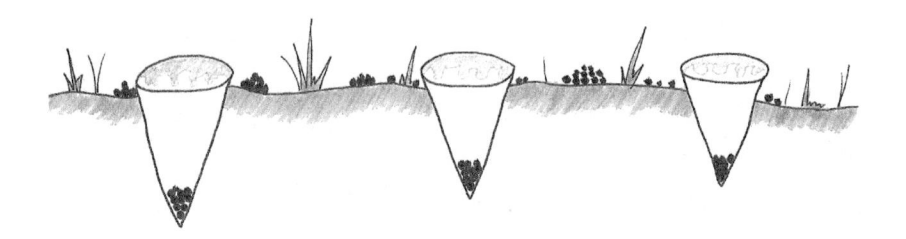

Stovepipe trap

Another trap that was used for pheasant or ground dwelling birds consisted of a length of pipe 8-10 inch in diameter and about 2 foot long, the trapper would keep one end open and the other end covered with mesh , bait was put throughout the trap and more toward the mesh end , the idea was the bird will push its way into the trap but cannot turn around or walk backwards to escape .
In the following picture is a roughly made stove pipe trap, i had to use what i had to hand to show you it , so instead of a stove pipe i used a thin plastic pipe but covered it in chicken wire to reinforce it.

MESH   TAPE   OPEN END

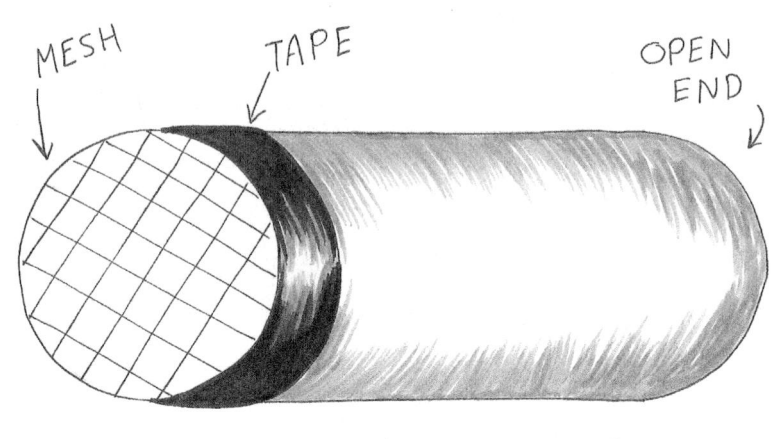

STOVE PIPE TRAP

53

String pheasant trap

The string bird trap consists of a stake pushed into the ground with berries, raisins, corn etc threaded onto strong thread or fishing line using a needle , the bait is placed at intervals of about a few inches ,the line is laid out and a pile of the bait is put at the end of the line . the idea is the bird will peck at the pile and start eating the string with bait on it , once the string is swallowed the bird is trapped and held in place by the string on the stake .

STRING PHEASANT TRAP

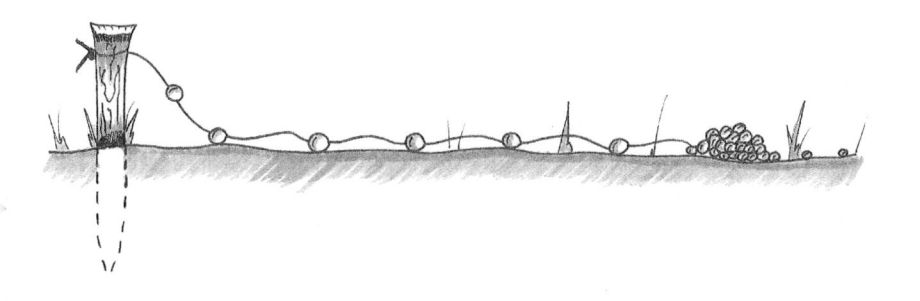

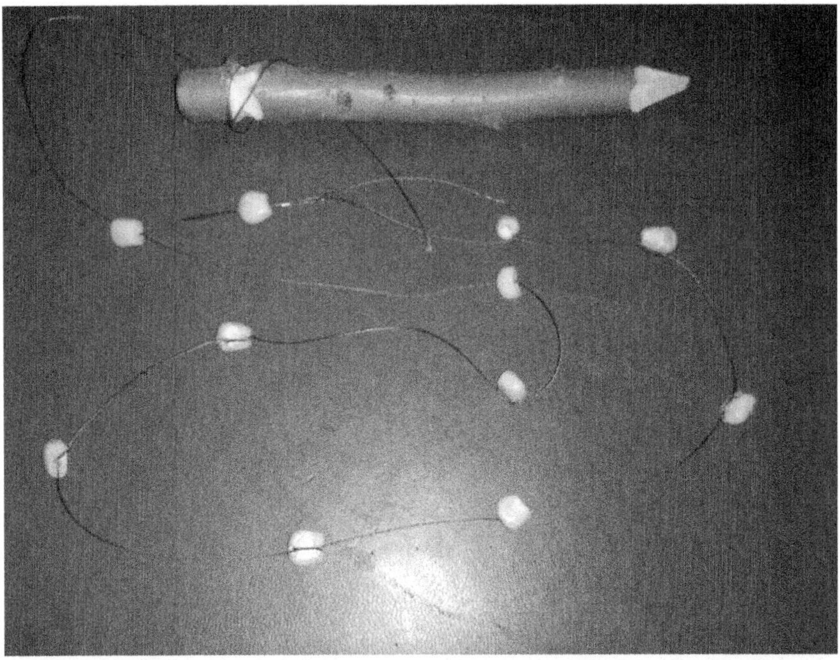

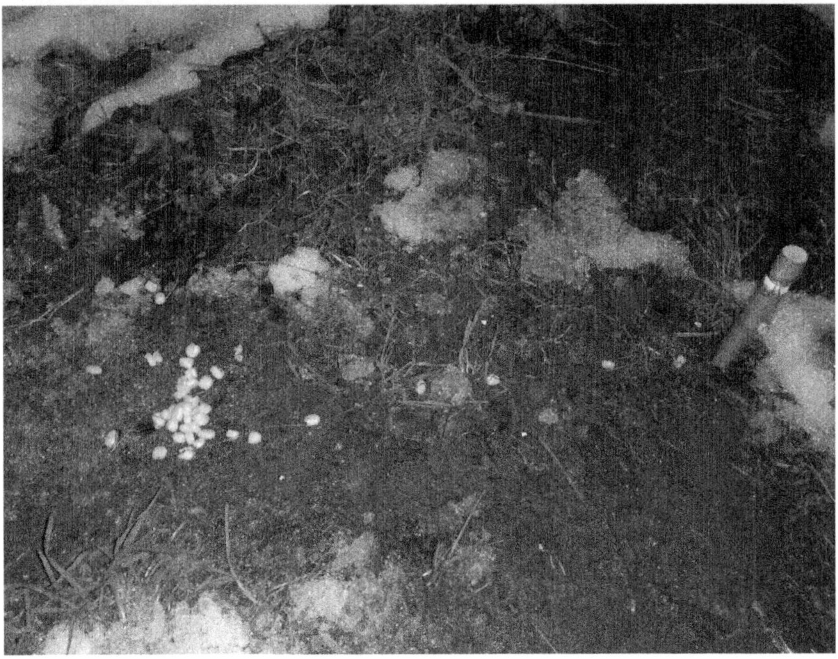

Snares

Whilst snaring pheasants was definitely frowned upon (and illegal) in the UK, the book wouldn't be complete without some mention of them .

The trappers and poachers of the old days would have used many different snares to catch pheasants most seemed to rely again on the the pheasant standing on a trigger to release the snare, but other snare traps were made by placing snares in holes in fences and under little arches that the pheasant would have to go under ,between each arch was branches etc to funnel the bird through the arch , on the following pages are a few different snare traps .

FOOT SNARE

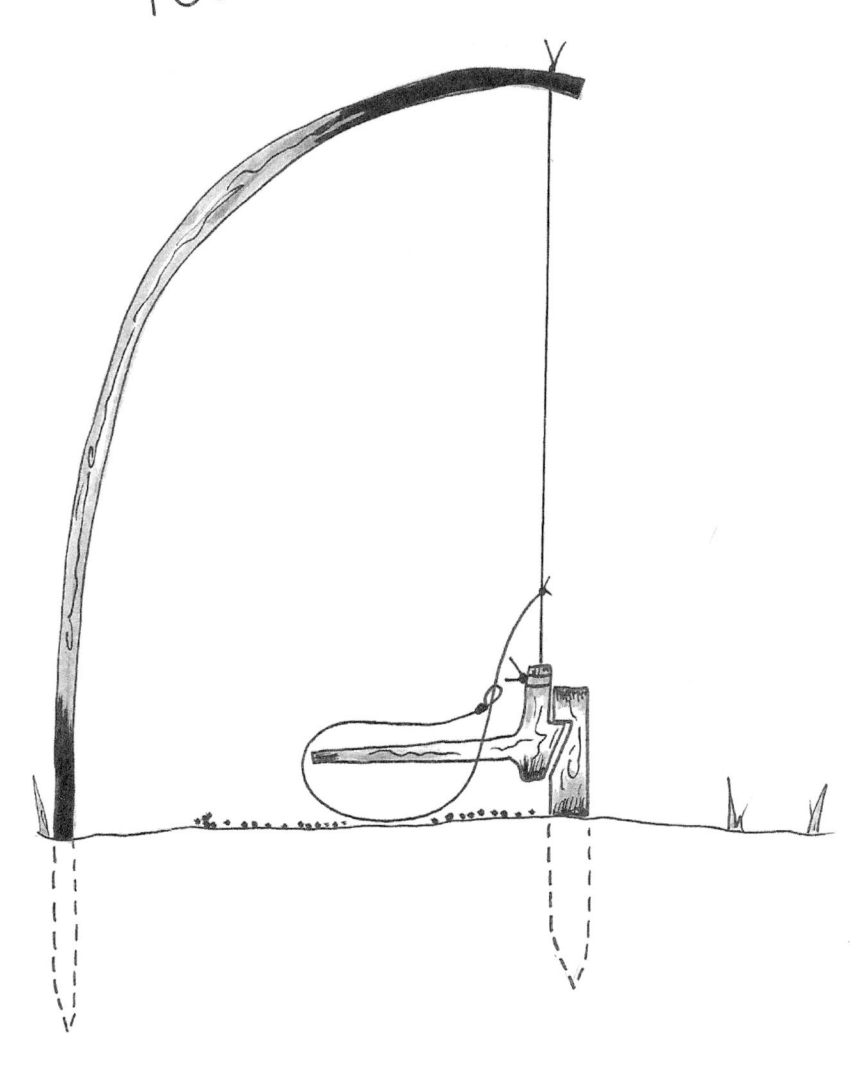

Primitive bird trap which relied upon the bird pecking at a stick with bait tied to it , which then released a toggle and snared the bird around the neck.

BIRD SNARES

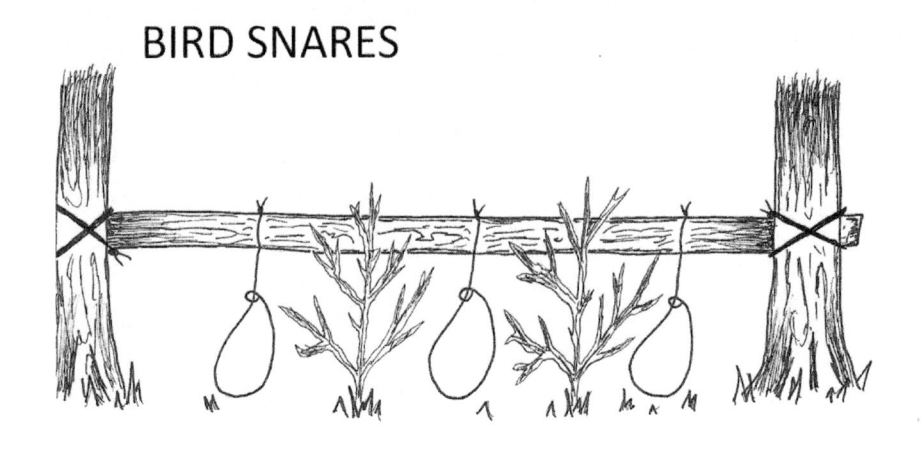

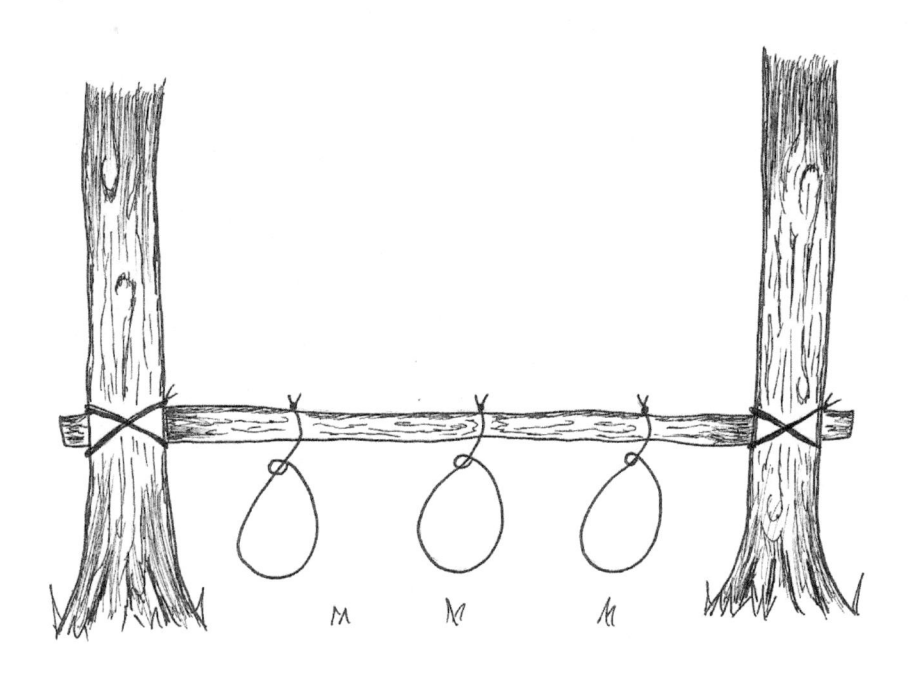

Toggle release snare trap, this one could work by catching the pheasant either around the neck if it pecks at the trigger or around the leg if it stand on the trigger

Other cage traps and triggers

No doubt in the old days they used many different traps and triggers on the following pages are a few to look at , most seemed to rely on the pheasant standing on a trigger rather than biting or chewing like primitive deadfall traps intended for mammals

Metal version of an 'old english cribbet trap'

The original versions would have been made from wood, the upright part of the trigger would have been a forked stick and the wire trigger would have been a bent stick .

A replica of a very old bird trap using a trigger that could have been used for pheasants , the lower part of the trigger on this one is string / rope.

Replica of a very old basket fall trap , with a larger cage this could easily catch pheasants, the trigger is string on this one too.

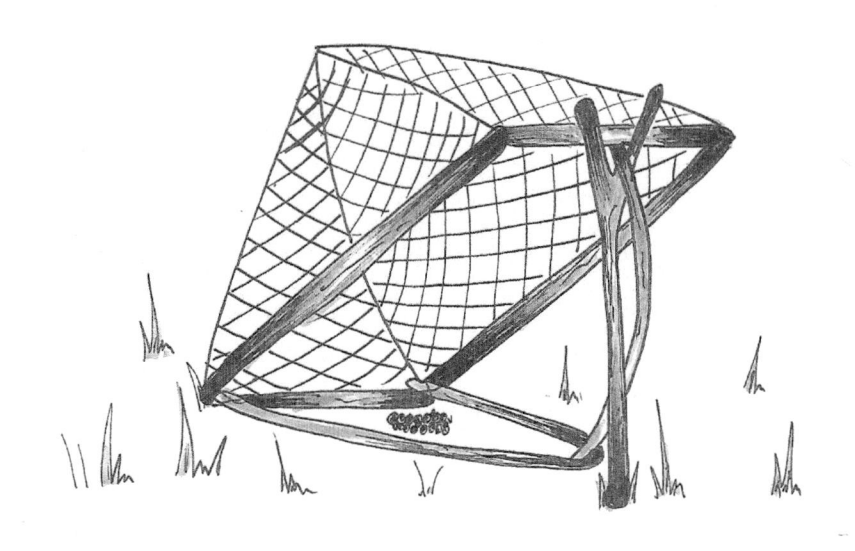

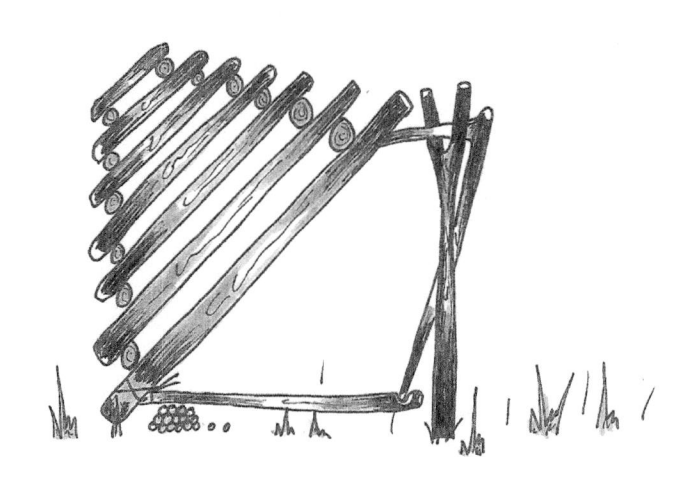

Top : old english cribbett type trap

Below : another variation of a trigger

Split stick triggers , above has a string.
Below has a branch as the trigger , both are cut / split in the middles to come apart.

Top : siberian deadfall trigger

Below: another split stick trigger with a stick inserted

Siberian type deadfall trigger

A similar trap to the pit trap, but using large split logs to make a box

One way door trap

The door on the cage is propped open with a stick , when the pheasant pushes its way in it dislodges the stick and door will close behind it and trap it inside the cage

Extra large drop door cage trap with a treadle plate inside, once the treadle plate is stood on the door drops down to catch the pheasant . a metal rod running from the treadle plate holds the door up . the doorway opening is about 1 foot x 1 foot drop door cage trap .

Many thanks for reading my book , i hope the info made sense, a lot of the history of these traps seems to have either been forgotten or kept a secret ,so it was very hard to add any relevant historic info , but i hope you enjoyed looking at the traps themselves . if you would like any further information check out my Youtube channel:
JJR SURVIVAL
10/2/2019

Also by the author :
Repurposed bushcraft equipment.
Bushcraft and survival hunting tools.
Basic survival traps.
Survival trapping, pheasant and ground bird traps.
How to make a natural slingshot
£160 bushcraft kit.
Practical homemade live traps
Simple mora knife modifications

Printed in Great Britain
by Amazon